CW01096174

"STOP THIRD PARTY DEBT COLLECTORS IN THEIR TRACKS"

Never Hear From Them Again!

BETH COLVETT

"STOP THIRD PARTY DEBT COLLECTORS IN THEIR TRACKS"

LEGAL DISCLAIMER

strategies presented in this ebook. We have no affiliation and imply no connotations with reference sites sponsored, maintained, created, edited or updated by: The Federal Trade Commission; Cornell University Law School; The Better Business Bureau; or The National Association of Attorney Generals.

We do not advocate any unlawful actions. We simply promote the law, as written, and as found within the information acquired. We cannot and do not give any legal or financial advice to any entity under any circumstances. We simply provide information, education, laws, codes, sources, cases, history, and other documentation to allow you the reader come to your own conclusions and pursue further research if you so desire.

We believe everyone should and **MUST** adhere to the Laws as they are written.

TABLE OF CONTENTS

LEGAL DISCLAIMER III

CONGRATULATIONS... VIII

WHO AM I? 1

IMPORTANT NOTE 3

What Is Unsecured And Secured Debt 3

What's So Bad About Third Party Debt Collection
Companies?..4

Stop Debt Collectors from Harassing You, Stop the
Calls...5

Bob's Bad Scenario 7

How to Send Third Party Debt Collectors Packing
and Never Hear From Them Again 9

Sample Debt Validation Letter 1.............................11

Sample Debt Validation Letter 2.............................17

Sample Debt Validation Letter 3.............................19

How to Send the Letter by Mail..............................24

Oh Yes, I Got Sued...24

My Friend Got Sued...26

Most All Collectors Try to Collect On Old, Outdated Debts 27

Statutes of Limitations on Debt by State.............29

WHY I DON'T LIKE DEBT SETTLEMENT COMPANIES.. 35

You Can Settle Your Own Debt With A Bank......37

Will My Credit Reports Be Harmed 38

Why I Would Never Borrow Against My Home To Pay Off Debt...38

Payday Loans and Tribal Lending..........................39

DEBT OPTIONS REVIEWED.. 41

Option #1: Bankruptcy...41

Option #2: Home Equity or Debt Consolidation Loan 42

Option #3: Debt Negotiation/Debt Settlement 43

Option #4: Credit Counseling...................................44

Option #5: Consolidation Overview.....................46

Check Your Credit Reports 48

INTERESTING INFORMATION, WEBSITES, AUDIOS AND BOOKS 51

CONGRATULATIONS

Congratulations for getting this book. I'm going to get to the "nitty-gritty" first since that's why you bought this book. I'll give you the fascinating info and interesting websites later for your personal education. Some of this new information for you is a bit startling!

If you're reading this book you need help combating the third party debt collectors who are hounding you. Third party debt collectors are companies that purchase alleged debts from your credit card banks, signature loan companies, hospitals, clearing houses, etc. We believe you should always pay your debts with the company you contracted with originally. If you owe a bank's credit card, signature loan, etc., pay it the best you can.

But...

Life gets in the way to all of us at one time or another and sometimes that means buying food for the kids before the creditors get paid. It is usually not our fault that we got into trouble, but life's circumstances and unforeseen emergencies happen. We think we should meet all our obligations if we can. There are a number of articles on the internet about paying off debt even with a low income.

WHO AM I?

Hello I'm Beth and I had a defining moment in my life in 2002 when I found my-self deep in credit card debt. My story is the same as millions of others. September 11th 2001, killed my electrolysis and permanent cosmetic business and after a year and a half, I found myself deep in credit card debt. We here in the US only paid what really needed to be paid and luxury items stalled out for quite a long time. Companies weren't hiring much either.

I needed help fast! I had a friend who had met a lady who worked with a debt relief company.

2

That company was a nationwide network of legal researchers, paralegals and genuinely caring people. I was so grateful for the help that came to me right when I needed it, I decided to work with this company to help others, too. I learned a lot!

The Federal Laws you'll want to read are The Fair Debt Collections Practices Act, The Fair Credit Billing Act, The Fair Credit Reporting Act and Truth in Lending Act. These are Federal Laws of the United States. Many countries like Canada, UK, and other countries have their own laws that work about the same.

IMPORTANT NOTE

WHAT IS UNSECURED AND SECURED DEBT

Unsecured debt is not secured by anything. In other words there is no type of property (your house, car, etc.) backing the loan. Credit cards and signature loans are unsecured. Your home and automobile are secured debts. If you default on a home or auto loan the bank can come and take back the car or home.

WHAT'S SO BAD ABOUT THIRD PARTY DEBT COLLECTION COMPANIES?

Third part debt collectors have merely purchased an alleged debt from your original creditor or from a clearing house. Sometimes these alleged debts are purchased in bundles. The **bad news** is that these debt collection companies, who prey on the uninformed, purchase these alleged debts for only "Pennies on the Dollar" and sometimes even less than a penny.

So for example, if you defaulted on a credit card account for $5,000, the debt collection company may have only paid $100 or $200 for it. Then they start calling the consumer and start harassing them to pay the full $5,000 plus interest. Does that sound fair?

Someone asked if you can contact the original bank to try and negotiate the original debt. Most times once an alleged debt has been sent off to a collection agency, the original creditor will have nothing more to do with that debt. This is why we call them third party debt collectors.

STOP DEBT COLLECTORS FROM HARASSING YOU, STOP THE CALLS.

First and foremost! I would never talk to a debt collector over the phone. Your "Rights" are never served over the phone. I used to tell them, "Send it in writing!" and then I would hang up. If you allow them to talk to you, many of the third party debt collection companies use scare tactics and make false statements to scare you into making a deal and paying them. Some of the lies they will tell you are:

- We're going to send the Sheriff to get you. You can be arrested.

- We can come and get your belongings, your home or your bank account.

- We're calling because you owe a debt. You know it and we don't have to prove anything.

- We're going to call your employer and garnish your wages.

- You have committed a crime by not paying this debt.

None of that is true. They just want you to admit that you owe a debt. They like it even better if you make a deal to pay them a little money. Then you're really hooked. I would never talk to anyone over the phone. If it's not in writing, it didn't happen.

You can see other violations in the Fair Debt Collections Practices Act. This is a Federal law and you can sue the third party debt collectors if they violate your rights in this law. This law is not intended for use with banks, credit card companies, auto loans, etc. Those companies are the original creditors. This law was created to prevent third party debt collection abuse.

See the law here: Fair Debt Collections Practices Act

BOB'S BAD SCENARIO

If Bob lives in Florida there is a four year statute of limitations on an open-ended accounts or credit card debts. If Bob defaulted on a credit card debt by making his last payment in March 30, 2002 the bank would likely have written it off by the end of September 2002. That debt would be dead by April 2006. A bank compliance officer that worked with us told me that after the bank writes it off, it gets sold out to the third party debt collectors.

In this scenario, Bob gets a call from a third party debt collector company that had purchased this alleged debt in 2009 (three years after the limit). If that company called Bob on the phone and threatened him, they would not really have any teeth, just bluster. BUT, if Bob didn't know the Fair Debt Collections Practices Act, a U.S. Law, and paid them a small amount, he just made a new contract with them. Then he's bound by that contract all over again. It's a whole new valid debt. They could even sue him in court. The debt collection company made an offer and Bob secured the contract with a small payment. That never had to happen.

HOW TO SEND THIRD PARTY DEBT COLLECTORS PACKING AND NEVER HEAR FROM THEM AGAIN

Anytime a third party debt collector would call me, I would say "Send it in Writing" and hang up the phone! Once a collector calls you, by law, they have five (5) days to send you a demand for payment letter. If not, that is a violation. When I would receive a letter (again I would never talk over the phone), I would send them a "Debt Validation Letter". This letter asks them to validate the alleged debt by proving there was a debt to begin with. I know, that sounds funny. BUT, 99 times out of 100 they cannot prove it! Even if they send you a few copies of statements, THAT IS NOT PROOF. Someone could have made copies of a statement and put your name on it. AND you never had a contract with the company calling you.

10

Most times the collector cannot get their hands on the original paperwork you may have signed with the original bank. Now days you can get a credit card account opened over the internet and never physically sign anything.

NOTE: Many law firms are now debt collection companies. I used the same letter (below) for them, too. After using these letters I never heard from any of the collectors again. A friend of mine used the first letter in a lawsuit and the plaintiff withdrew the case. There are three sample letters below.

SAMPLE DEBT VALIDATION LETTER 1

DATE   CERTIFIED MAIL RECEIPT # XXXX

[COLLECTION AGENCY]
ATTN: [Collection Manager or NAME OF PARTY]
[Street Address]
[City], [State] [Zip Code]

Your File Number XXXX-XXXX- XXXX-XXXX

Non-Negotiable Non-Transferable
NOTICE OF DISPUTE
Applicable to All Successors and Assigns

Dear Collection Manager:

I am in receipt of an unsigned form letter perpetrating a claim from [CREDIT CARD COMPANY] in the amount of $[xx,xxx.xx]. This Notice is not a refusal to pay. This Notice constitutes my Demand to Cease and Desist Collection Activities Prior to Validation under oath (verification) of the Purported Debt. Furthermore, this Notice confirms that your claim is disputed under 15 USC § 1692 et seq.

Please verify under oath that this claim is valid, free from any claims and defenses including but not limited to any breach of agreement, failure of consideration, and material alteration of the original agreement. Further, that the alleged account was transferred in good faith and by the consent of all parties involved.

"verification, n. 1. A formal declaration made in the presence of an authorized officer, such as a notary public, by which one swears to the truth of the statements in the document. ..." Black's Law Dictionary, 7th Edition (1999).

"It is established law that a verification is a sworn statement of the truth of the facts stated in the instrument which is verified." H.A.M.S.

Company v. Electric Contractors of Alaska, Inc. (1977) 563 Pacific Reporter 258, 260.

In addition you are hereby requested to produce the following documents:

1. A front and back, true and correct copy of the alleged signed agreement

2. The name, address and title of the officer that retained you

3. Proof of debt

4. Proof of Identification of Creditor

5. Proof of Identification of Debtor

6. A copy of the contract or document where I willingly and knowingly affixed my authorized signature, making me liable for any alleged debt to your client

7. A copy of your license to be a Collection Agency in the State of [State]

8. A copy of your license to operate as a collection agency in the State of [State]

9. A copy of the implementing regulation instructing you on your duties, obligations, authority, and limitations of authority

10. A copy of the law giving you authority to use the U.S. Mails to make ethereal and unsubstantiated claims of amounts due you or your client

11. The bond with account #, trustee of said account, and my right to sue said account for any violations to the [State] Business and Commercial Code while you are attempting to operate a business in [State]

Failure to present every item 1-11 in the above documentation and verification in thirty-days

(30) will invalidate your presentment under the laws, statutes, and subsequent commercial codes of the State of [State], and Federal Law.

All communications and omissions will be made part of and incorporated into any litigation arising from this matter and all Fair Debt Collection Practices Act violations will be dealt with accordingly. You must contact me in writing and request an extension in the event that you need more than thirty-days (30) to verify and validate the debt. Failure to do so confirms that the time limit is reasonable.

Notice to the Principal is Notice to the Agent, and Notice to the Agent is Notice to the Principal.

NOTICE

THIS IS NOT A REQUEST FOR CONFIRMATION THAT YOU HAVE A COPY OF AN AGREEMENT OR COPIES OF STATEMENTS. THIS IS A DEMAND FOR PROOF THAT YOU HAVE THE REQUISITE KNOWLEDGE OF THE FACTS, THAT YOU PROVIDE A VERIFICATION; AND THAT THE ALLEGED CREDITOR PROVIDED ADEQUATE CONSIDERATION AND INCURRED A FINANCIAL LOSS UNDER THE FULL & COMPLETE ORIGINAL AGREEMENT.

Signed without prejudice

By [Name]

SAMPLE DEBT VALIDATION LETTER 2

Date   Certified Mail #xxxx xxxx xxxx xxxx xxxx – Return Receipt Requested

Debt Collection Company
Address
City Sate Zip

Re: Your File Number: xxxxxxxxx

Greetings; Thank you for your recent inquiry. This is not a refusal to pay, but a notice that your claim is disputed. On [DATE] I received your communication in a letter [dated].

This is a request for validation made pursuant to the Fair Debt Collection Practices Act. Please be advised that I am not requesting a "verification" that you have my mailing address, I am requesting a "validation:" that is, competent evidence that I have some contractual obligation to pay you.

18

I dispute the alleged debt in its entirety. I demand that you provide me with a complete chain of title to the alleged debt including: the name and address of the original creditor, the name and address of any and all subsequent creditors, the name and address of the current creditor, and complete validation of the amount of the alleged debt.

Your failure to satisfy this request within the requirements of the Fair Debt Collection Practices Act will be construed as your absolute waiver of any and all claims against me, and your tacit agreement to compensate me for costs and attorney's fees.

Sincerely,

Name

SAMPLE DEBT VALIDATION LETTER 3

To whom it may concern:

Please note that that this is not a refusal to pay off the account, but a notice sent as per the Fair Debt Collection practices Act, 15 USC 1692g Sec. 809 (b). The notice states that your claim is disputed and validation of the account is required.

This notice is not a request for verification of the account or proof of my mailing address, but a request for validation made pursuant to the FDCPA laws. I humbly request that your agency/office sends me valid proof that I am legally obligated to pay you.

Please provide me with the below mentioned things:

- The amount you claim I owe you

- Explain and show me how you have computed the amount

- Send me the copies of any documents that prove I agreed to pay the alleged amount

- Identify the original creditor

- Confirm that the account has not crossed the SOL period

- Prove that you're a licensed debt collector

- Show me your license numbers and registered agent.

I would like to inform you that in case your agency has reported invalidated account information to any of the 3 main Credit Bureau's such as TransUnion, Equifax, Experian, then it will be regarded as a fraudulent action under both the federal and state laws. Due to this reason, if any negative item is reported to any of my credit reports by your agency or the agency that you represent, then I will be compelled to take legal steps against you for the below mentioned reasons:

- Violation of the FCRA

- Violation of the FDCPA

- Defamation of character

If your agency can provide me with the requested documents, I will need minimum 30 days to investigate this information, and during this period of time, all collection activities must be stopped.

I would like to further inform you that if any action is taken (during the validation period) which could be regarded as detrimental to any of my credit reports, then I will seek advice from my attorney for lawsuit. This includes listing any information on a credit report that could be incorrect or invalidated, or confirming an account as correct when in fact there is no provided proof that it is.

If your agency/company fails to respond to this debt validation request within a period of 30 days from the date of your receipt, then the account information must be completely deleted from my credit report, and a copy of such deletion request should be sent to me at once.

I would also like to request, in writing, that no calls should be made by your agency or company at my residence or work place. If your agency attempts to make unlimited or computer generated calls to me or any third parties, then it will be considered harassment, and I will have no option but to file lawsuit. All future communications with me should be done in writing and sent to the address mentioned in this letter.

It would be advisable that you assure that your records are in order before I am forced to take legal action. This is an attempt to correct your records, any information obtained shall be used for that purpose.

Sincerely,

Your Signature

Your Name

NOTE: There are other letters on the internet that you can use as sample validation letters. Just go to Google and search for "debt validation letter".

HOW TO SEND THE LETTER BY MAIL

When a consumer sends any correspondence to a debt collector or law firm it is a must that the letter be sent "Certified" with a return receipt request attached. The post office can provide the two small forms needed. The reason for this is to prevent a debt collector from saying that they did not receive the debt validation letter.

OH YES, I GOT SUED

Back in 2007, before I knew this information, a third party debt collection agency sued me in a court of law regarding a credit card debt. I lost, of course, and a judgment was issued against me. If I knew then what I know now, I could have nipped that in the bud!!!

I found out later that the judgment had been sold over and over several times. A debt collection company had purchased the judgment and almost ten (10) years later, I got a letter from them. I would still demand validation. If that judgment has been sold over and over, I think it would be pretty hard for a collector to validate it and supply the "chain of title".

Another interesting thing is that one of my friends got a paper in the mail from a third party debt collector that looked like a real court document. It looked just like a valid court case/complaint and it looked like it had been filed in the name of the bank. My friend called the court to ask about it and found out that the court had no record of that lawsuit. It had not been filed in the court. Then she checked with the original bank and the alleged debt had been written off some time back. The bank had nothing to do with that lawsuit. I think that's pretty sneaky and underhanded.

Note: Having said that, before a suit ever happens, a debt collector must contact you and send you a dunning letter (a demand to pay). When I would send my favorite letter (letter number one above), I would never hear from them again. Sometime later, a different collector would contact me on the same alleged debt. The first company just sold it after the validation letter was received because they knew they couldn't sue or collect.

MY FRIEND GOT SUED

A friend of mine got sued by a debt collection company in his state. They filed the complaint in his town with is about 350 miles away from their office. A law firms must place a lawsuit in the consumers home town.

My friend used some of the verbiage from a "Demand for Validation" letter number one in his answer to the complaint. Several weeks later he received a letter from that law firm saying that they had withdrawn the case. That really opened our eyes.

MOST ALL COLLECTORS TRY TO COLLECT ON OLD, OUTDATED DEBTS

I don't know how many times I've received letters from collection agencies demanding that I pay them on a debt that was past the statute of limitations for my state. Each state has a statute that states a time limit on certain types of debts.

In other words, credit card debt has an expiration date. In Texas after four years from the time of the last payment I was able to make, a debt collector cannot sue me for that alleged debt.

That doesn't keep the third party debt collectors from buying and trying to collect on old debts. They are hoping that the consumer doesn't know the statutes and the FDCPA law.

For example, if a collector called someone in Alaska on an alleged credit card debt that was six years old, that debt is three years past the statute of limitations for that state. The collector is really out of luck if the consumer knows that the alleged debt died three years before.

STATUTES OF LIMITATIONS ON DEBT BY STATE

State	Written Contracts	Oral Contracts	Promissory Notes	Open-Ended Accounts (Including Credit Cards)
Alabama	3	6	6	3
Alaska	3	6	3	3
Arizona	6	3	5	3
Arkansas	5	3	3	5
California	4	2	4	4
Colorado	6	6	6	6
Connecticut	6	3	6	6
Delaware	3	3	3	3
D.C.	3	3	3	3
Florida	5	4	5	4
Georgia	6	4	6	4 or 6**

State	Written Contracts	Oral Contracts	Promissory Notes	Open-Ended Accounts (Including Credit Cards)
Hawaii	6	6	6	6
Idaho	5	4	5	5
Illinois	10	5	10	5 or 10***
Indiana	10	6	10	6
Iowa	10	5	5	10
Kansas	3	3	3	3
Kentucky	15	5	15	5 or 15****
Louisiana	3	10	10	3
Maine	6	6	6	6
Maryland	3	3	6	3
Massachusetts	6	6	6	6
Michigan	6	6	6	6

State	Written Contracts	Oral Contracts	Promissory Notes	Open-Ended Accounts (Including Credit Cards)
Minnesota	6	6	6	6
Mississippi	3	3	3	3
Missouri	5	5	5	5
Montana	8	5	8	8
Nebraska	4	4	4	4
Nevada	4	4	4	4
New Hampshire	3	3	3	3
New Jersey	6	6	6	6
New Mexico	4	4	4	4
New York	6	6	6	6
North Carolina	3	3	5	3
North Dakota	6	6	6	6

State	Written Contracts	Oral Contracts	Promissory Notes	Open-Ended Accounts (Including Credit Cards)
Ohio	6	6	6	6
Oklahoma	5	3	5	3 or 5****
Oregon	6	6	6	6
Pennsylvania	4	4	4	4
Rhode Island	10	10	10	10
South Carolina	10	10	3	3
South Dakota	6	3	6	6
Tennessee	6	6	6	6
Texas	4	4	4	4
Utah	6	4	6	4
Vermont	5	3	6	3
Virginia	6	6	5	6

State	Written Contracts	Oral Contracts	Promissory Notes	Open-Ended Accounts (Including Credit Cards)
Washington	6	3	6	6
West Virginia	10	10	10	10
Wisconsin	6	6	10	6
Wyoming	10	8	10	8

** Georgia Court of Appeals came out with a decision on January 24, 2008 in Hill v. American Express that in Georgia the statute of limitations on a credit card is six years after the amount becomes due and payable. *** An Illinois appeals court ruled on May 20, 2009, that the statute of limitations on a credit card debt without a written contract was 5 years. **** State law doesn't specify the limitations on open accounts. Source: Bankrate.com

34 BETH COLVETT

WHY I DON'T LIKE DEBT SETTLEMENT COMPANIES

D ebt settlement companies probably don't want you to know about this.

I contacted a debt settlement company that was advertising on the internet. I won't mention any names, but I'll call this company "ABC Company". The man I spoke with said that they could reduce my credit card debt by about 50%. When they added their fee on top of the 50%, it turned into about 65% to 70%. Then I found out that their fee would be paid before they would begin paying my so-called creditors.

If it was going to take almost a year to pay their fee before they started paying the creditors. The **BIG PROBLEM** with this, I'm told, is that many banks write off an account if they can't collect on it within 180 days (six months). A bank compliance officer told me that if the bank writes off an account, they sell it off to third party debt collectors or to a debt clearing house.

If the debt settlement company (ABC Company) isn't paying the original bank, after their fee was paid, they would be paying a third party debt collector. In my way of thinking, if I don't have a contract with a third party debt collector, then I don't own them the full amount of the alleged debt! I suppose that "ABC Company" would negotiate the amount down some.

Remember that the third party debt collectors only paid pennies on the dollar for these alleged debts. Then they want a consumer to pay the whole original amount plus interest. I don't know about you, but I don't think that's fair.

The same goes for debt consolidation companies.

YOU CAN SETTLE YOUR OWN DEBT WITH A BANK

One of the paralegal ladies from the company I worked with back in 2003 told me that if a bank cannot collect a debt within 6 months of the last payment, they must write it off if they want to get their tax credit and insurance. That's hearsay so I'm not sure if that's true for everyone, but it seemed true for me.

I noticed that one of my credit card bank accounts was nearing the 6 month mark. I mean I was not able to make payments for six months. I received a letter one day around the fourth month saying that the bank would take 50% and call it even. Right before the six month mark, I received a letter that the bank would take 25% of the amount.

WILL MY CREDIT REPORTS BE HARMED

Yes. Sometimes I wonder if having "Credit" got me into trouble in the first place. From what I saw, the bad marks on my credit report stayed for only seven years. Thankfully I now have very good credit after years of paying debt on time. Granted, I kept the credit card debt very low and make double payments. You can get there, too.

WHY I WOULD NEVER BORROW AGAINST MY HOME TO PAY OFF DEBT

Your home is one of your most important assets. If I were to borrow against my home and something terrible happened and I couldn't pay my debts, I would lose my home. Many states have homestead laws that protect your home against debt collection.

PAYDAY LOANS AND TRIBAL LENDING

This information is not to be used with these types of lenders. With Payday loans the consumer must submit a check to the creditor to hold. They are an "original creditor".

Tribal lenders are based on Tribal Lands and provide short term or payday loans. They also lend for housing, education and sometime health care.

40 BETH COLVETT

DEBT <u>OPTIONS REVIEWED</u>

There are many things to consider when contemplating your debt situation. Please take time and review the debt relief alternatives listed below as these will help you determine which option best suits your needs. I did not want to use these options, but they are included here for information.

OPTION #1: BANKRUPTCY

A bankruptcy can stay on your credit report for seven to ten years (dependent on the type of bankruptcy and state obtained). It can make it very difficult to obtain future credit, buy a home or car and sometimes even get a job. Almost every creditor, lender, and employer asks if you have ever filed bankruptcy. Due to the severity of this option it should always be considered as a last resort. Bankruptcy Info.

OPTION #2: HOME EQUITY OR DEBT CONSOLIDATION LOAN

This option may work if you have good credit and a large amount of equity in your home. However, please remember that by going this route you will convert your unsecured debt (credit cards, etc.) into secured debt, which puts your home in jeopardy. If something was to happen and payments are missed or late, you could lose your home. Also consider that if some other emergency came up and you needed some money, where will you turn if your equity is already used up? In addition, when establishing credit, more often than not, you will be advised by a financial planner that applying for a home equity or debt consolidation loan should be a last resort to remedy any negative financial situation. Don't turn your home into Debt!

OPTION #3: DEBT NEGOTIATION/DEBT SETTLEMENT

These companies will negotiate for you with the creditors. Usually they will negotiate the debt down to around 35%-50%. <u>They are only legal in some states!</u> Their fee is usually 15% of the total amount of debt that you have. They will have you save up money in your own account or have you send them the money to save for you (in this case they will make the interest on your money). When an amount is settled upon with the creditor, the settlement company will send a lump sum to zero out the account. **There's One**

Big Problem: They neglect to tell you that you could be sued later by a debt collector.

OPTION #4: CREDIT COUNSELING

Also known as Debt Management Programs (DMPs) or Debt Consolidation Programs. These programs typically take about 5-7 years to complete. You are usually charged a setup/enrollment fee in addition to monthly service fees for the duration of the program. Most companies also pressure you to make 'voluntary contributions', another way to obtain more fees. Credit counseling companies TRY to get creditors to lower their interest rates. Even if your interest rates are lowered, most creditors will actually require your minimum monthly payment to be much higher than it was before in exchange. You are required to send your monthly payments to the credit counseling company, NOT directly to your own creditors. Because of the way this type of program is designed, the following negative outcomes occur more often than you may think: Even if you are never late or miss a payment to a credit counseling company, don't forget that once they receive your payment they are in control of your money. Unfortunately, this means any mistakes, computer 'glitches', etc. can alter the day your creditors receive payment. Many creditors have strict policies on dropping you from their program when payments are late or missed REGARDLESS of whose 'fault' it was. After being dropped, you must start making your own payments to the Credit Card Company or bank all over again. If the bank or finance company does not receive a payment within six months, they will write if off their books and sell it off to 3rd part debt collectors (you don't want to deal with these nasty people). Credit counseling companies are considered as a 3rd party agent, in control of your debt and money, and will appear on your credit report as a 3rd party mark. This is typically viewed as an equivalent to Chapter 13 Bankruptcy.

OPTION #5: CONSOLIDATION OVERVIEW

The purpose of consolidation is to bring together all your existing credit cards, store cards, personal loans, and overdraft debts into one single loan or under one umbrella (agency). Since the individual is already having difficulty, the credit record will reflect this as well. This results in a consumer loan with a relatively high interest rate. The payment is lower than the total being paid currently, however, the length of time to pay off the loan is significantly longer. This will take several years. Some consolidation companies advertise their program will take 10 years. This is actually based on the loan period, and the fact you must keep the monthly payments current.

Consolidation usually includes credit counseling through a credit-counseling agency of some type. Credit-counseling agencies primarily negotiate unsecured debt, such as credit cards, installment loans, retail finance plans, medical bills and personal debts. Contrary to popular belief, credit-counseling agencies cannot force creditors to accept their proposals. Unlike a lender providing a "debt consolidation loan," when consumers consolidate their debt through a nonprofit credit-counseling agency, the agency does not then become the creditor. In this regard, the agency is, in essence, a conduit for disbursing payments to their client's creditors.

The last form of consolidation is a Debt Reduction Settlement. This is a process used by both debtors and creditors to settle a debt for less than what is owed. The process is also called Third Party Debt Negotiation. If negotiated properly on behalf of the debtor, it can reduce the consumer's debt.

I've been told that settlements typically range from 40% to 80% of the current debt, with the typical debt settled for around 50%. After a year, sometimes two, the individual in Consolidation has not reduced his debt significantly. If a loan was secured with equity from the home, this property is further tied up by a second mortgage. Usually, the consolidation consumer ends up choosing Bankruptcy.

CHECK YOUR CREDIT REPORTS

Every year you can get all three of your credit reports from Experian, Equifax, and TransUnion from https://www.annualcreditreport.com/index.action this is the only site authorized by Federal Law. This site it totally free. In other words you don't have to purchase anything to get a copy of your credit report like the companies that advertise on television.

In Conclusion, I hope you gained some <u>relief</u> and some "peace of mind" after reading this information. Don't let the debt collectors scare you. They just want to bluff you out of your hard earned money. You might want to read this short book again several times so you really understand the **power** that is contained here. We and our company learned this the hard way. Now you can be assured that it has been tested and works.

50 BETH COLVETT

INTERESTING INFORMATION, WEBSITES, AUDIOS AND BOOKS

"The Money Masters" is a brilliant video about the how money was created and how the Federal Reserve works. Don't miss this fascinating historical documentary.
http://www.themoneymasters.com/the-money-masters/

"The Creature from Jekyll Island, A Second Look at The Federal Reserve" Audio CD: "An Address by G. Edward Griffin. Here is a close look at the Money Magicians' mirrors and smoke machines, the pulleys, cogs, and wheels that create the grand illusion called money. Based on Mr.

Griffin's book of the same title. Deep discount on Activist Package."
https://realityzone.com/product/creature-from-jekyll-island-lecture-1-cd/

"Two Faces of Debt" is a booklet is the fifth revision of "Debt - Jeckyl and Hyde," originally published by the Federal Reserve Bank of Chicago in the November 1953 issue of its monthly review.
https://www.scribd.com/document/192190186/Federal-Reserve-Bank-Two-Faces-of-Debt

United States Federal Consumer Laws:

- The Fair Debt Collections Practices Act
- The Fair Credit Billing Act
- The Fair Credit Reporting Act
- Truth in Lending Act

Printed in Great Britain
by Amazon